For Emил

WALT WHITMAN
AND OTHER POEMS

love

Dic

1.01.08

Dic Edwards

WALT WHITMAN

AND OTHER POEMS

OBERON BOOKS
LONDON

First published in 2007 by Oberon Books Ltd

521 Caledonian Road, London N7 9RH

Tel: 020 7607 3637 / Fax: 020 7607 3629

email: info@oberonbooks.com

www.oberonbooks.com

A catalogue record for this book is available from the British Library.

ISBN: 978-1-84002-814-0

Printed in Great Britain by Antony Rowe Ltd, Chippenham.

This book is for Gwenda, my wife

Acknowledgements

Thanks to Torben for his wonderful plays;
for his lobbying and his editing

Thanks to Justin for the climbing and the editing help

Thanks to Keith Burstein for his often sublime music

CONTENTS

WALT WHITMAN

For James Hogan

I found a starling standing
on a pebble in Georgia by the Black Sea
where the Caucasus root for water
where I was rooting for the word
where the starling roots his home
nesting in holes in walls and under eaves
and in the nest boxes those brave of bone to bone
democracy have put in the fields.
And the starling feeds on insects and feeds its young also
on insects as the world feeds
on the sacrifice made by insects
and all those who make that sacrifice
and also the worms that churn the soil
in the civil war of earth with Earth
and make bread of Earth
its only competition being with night to bring sun
to the churned earth where the waters
we root for will sink and make a salad of soil.

With this thought I turn my mind to that other Georgia
where on the banks of the Savannah
I see a man – Whitman – whose tears feed the river along
which Sherman's army in his Civil War rages
and whose beard all tousled tobacco is a gift
for the young men for all young men to take in their mouths and chew
like worms chew with their ballet the earth;
I see this man watching
the tearful army in baritone bouldering the Savannah to Savannah
and as they are crushed like insects
he weaves of leaves like a starling's nest
the nesting bed of the American canon
wet with the waters that will make an adobe of the leaves and small muds
the waters that drain the land of scourge
and feed the Cyclops eye of the
Gulf of Mexico whose lash fans the soft cheek of the Earth.

ON CADER IDRIS

See me in the mountain's loom
where the cold furnishes
the inchoate mind's rooms
with shale dishes;

see me, heroic, high
in the furious mist
where the two faced sky
aches to kiss
the flocked soul
foraging for bliss;

and maybe see me die tonight
as the ice packs
the scorched hand
of the old god hack
and that glum moon
a clock with hands
that honey the night
in spoonfuls to mock.

But below the women feed
graves their stiffened words
as babies bleed
to fill god's unfleshed gourds;

you will not see that child gotten
from my torn roots
down the forgotten
line where the train hoots
the owl home lamed
and the light down the road
that swings damned
like a load
torch in the hand

of one who prays terrified
of the sucking god.

And you will not see your children
dragging their proletarian cart
through the streets of heaven
where the dogs of good eat hearts.

SERENDIPITY

I had often hated my father
for his Rightist politics
much, maybe,
as McCarthy had hated the Leftward Rosenbergs for theirs,
so it was shocking how
I first came across the Rosenbergs on Discovery the night
the old man died; learnt how Ethel
had decorated like a laurel wreath
that chair that had written the book
on temporariness;
how they'd had to kill her
three times: too short
to ride the executioner's practised
route to hell.
                    Her killing
had haunted me all through Dad's
obsequies. At the time
of his burning I had imagined him with her in
a lonely hotel with a sign for
Harry's chops and sweet relish. She
was there to look for her bleached boys somewhere
in the bulging gulp of ever.

I imagined him saying to her:
"Jesus, Ethel! It's
as if you've made your wedding with electricity
something you could believe in.
                              The whole world has said:
save yourself! Think of the kids! Give
a name, any name! Make one up!
And you'd said: no!"
"Yes!" she says: "If I cannot with dignity combat their cowardly
rhetoric, I cannot be human.
I'll go! I'll tell the boys: don't worry, we all
walk that red carpet to the sea."

When I got Dad's ashes, I put them
into the car boot. I thought what a hoot
Ethel was. While imagining my old man
now marooned beyond politics' pale
in the boneless silence out of which both he and Ethel
had sprung when born
bubbles of flesh and ifs, her I imagined
as she received that final hit
feeling Julius exploding in her one more time
as she fried, and as I shut the boot
of my car
I heard her post sex sigh
la, la, la, la, la, la, la
as though swept up in that melt
of nourishing death Virginia Woolf had felt.

PLATHDAY

From the common-mussel shore
we drove north to the moors

through the night
in the gulf of the rain
the vain wan warning light
the hooked bird
the heard smack.

Heptonstall upon the ice
of high Yorkist moors
adrift of those driftwood cadres
the late poets.

In the streets
the cold wind of the devil's sleeping
the broken white line and the corner stone
the pole with notice of death's presence
the drift of too early night before a lamplight
the gargoyle in the frightening
architecture of ruin
no footpath even to evening

and Plath's bitched-over, desultory grave
the size of it the measure
of her reputation at her interment

and from within

the tap of the fabled bird
upon the diamond pile of eternity.

COMING OF AGE (in 7s)

In Monaco shivering
like a tattered flag in a
mistral donkey coat upon
a rack of shoulders I ate
the fillet steak flesh of filched
apples outside a convent's
gates which secured an Eden

of girls fecund with foolish
vim. They must have known I was
an atheist but not that
I was asexual in
that cold ready to sell my
ass. That night, I surrendered
to the police for a bed

behind bars, the innocence
of my capitulation
intriguing like eccentric
sex. Midnight my mother prays
at my feet; next night I am
in the cold hall of Lyons
Central, penniless, teasing

possibilities from the
clipped narrative offered by
the Trojan hunters. One man,
perhaps an Arab slaver
trader in boy flesh eyes me.
He will pray at my feet; buy
me chocolates and keep me

warm in his curled lap with
concupiscent smile. He takes
me to a midnight café
where boys with eyes painted to
evoke the mysterious
lust of catamites eye me
and old men in white suits pimp

my space. We eat the root of
the unsoiled lotus and drink
the blood of carnal fruit. He
takes me towards a house, a
room, a bed. I imagine
the pounding at my back and…
that fear of slipping; in a

second I turn, run and in
turn one way then the other
cross bridges of the Rhone from
my dangerous edge; bridges
connecting my life's ages
like branches in the ghost tree
of an ageless deception.

WIFE

On the way to Cornwall for a few days
my wife says: let's stop off at
your Mother's, I need the toilet. My mother's
not there now – she's with brother Bryn for her
endgame. No, our boy's in the house – hardly
a boy. We go in and what I'm
confronted with is, in the rooms where once
mother languished – not to put too
fine a point on it – a slaughter house.

I lost it. I said:
                    this place is a bit of a mess.
He swore at me. The boy.
                              On the M4 I called
him the worst thing I could. To the wife. I couldn't
help it. I was enraged – he was like this when he was
5! He's a c...! (A word he'd use and, look at me,
I don't have the courage to name it in the privacy
of this confessional!)
                        She doesn't deserve this. It's her son.
She is distraught. She can't understand. What was
the matter with me? How do you explain? I can't.
But I knew her feeling – those moments when it
feels as if everything has fallen apart and you can't
even name the constituent parts to rebuild. Then
we were silent and in the silence I apologised to
an abstraction of her (I couldn't actually say it)
and the boy. And everyone from my past and all
those who would come pointlessly
after me.
            Pointlessly.
                          It had come to this. How have
I become so pessimistic?
                          Is it because it won't stop raining?
No! Because I can't get the bathroom door to stay shut?

No! No!
           Because we will never stop the middle classes
sending working class kids to war while they send theirs
to college? More like that, yes. And these things
are what you might call the sub-text to my anger.
And after, of course, mostly because
I'd shattered her peaceful morning once again with my
fanaticism. That phoney physical morality of
cleanliness; of putting everything in order
like a complete naming of things.
                          (Could
this be the writer in me?)

A night or two later, we're sitting on the patio
of a small hotel on the edge of Bodmin Moor. So:
in my mind I still have the stuff with the boy;
           over my shoulder
the empty prowling moor
                      and before me my vulnerable
petite wife like a child cradling her one arm
                     - plastered to
the elbow with her broken thumb –
in her other and in her lovely eyes, for a moment
                     – at least
as I perceived it –
something like loss and over
to the West over the North Cornish coast
a huge black cloud promoting twilight and
sadness.
           Above it, alone in a narrow band of
rapidly thinning blue is Venus.
                          She said: when I was
a kid I knew all the planets. We were silent for
a moment.
           And then, we tried as one, desperately

for what could have been our last ever hour on Earth if
you think of it
    as the light failed to name them.
        And we just couldn't.
I gulped my drink down. I must have looked close
to despair for she said: relax.
It doesn't matter. You can look it up. Get another drink.
Then she took my hand in her broken one and said:
you know how the blue brings out the blue
in someone's eyes?
       Well that bit of Venus sky
is bringing out the pacific blue in yours.

DEMOCRACY

Today, to escape the news, you drive over the Northern hills
where the pines are like the great
Californian Redwood
already a thousand years old as The West began.

As you climb out of Pontrhydygroes
the road holding to the sky like string to a kite
your mind cradled in an Oglala's skull,
you see that these hills and times
belong to the vast sea-prairies of the imagination

and you imagine over the summit
Baghdad: that war that you can't escape;
man is small and mean: no more than
a filing of lava caught on the tail of Darwin's iguana

and war is the proof of that meanness and pettiness
it comes from the foolish importance we place on events in our time
even to the extent that we may let our parliaments
become warehouses for the dying
with thousands of beds
soup kitchens and refrigerated rooms
cattle, sheep and pig stables
bakeries of a thousand loaves and a brewery;
and it may be that in the end you can pass the time here
in a kind of peace fed on the passing of life.

Not in the news, a woman in Sacramento has a morning dove
come to her window sill;
she imagines her husband killed in the war
she yesterday waved him off to
and her soft stupid tears fall –
into the darkness that predates his being.

A TWILIGHT IN AMERICA

The air was heavy over L.A.
that morning. I remember thinking: my first sip

of mother's milk is the moment
suicide begins. So that's that. That's where it all started.

I thought of the yachts in Hyannis; mother's
sun-dried breasts like the white hills of the desert;

I dreamed of drinking dry the sea off Cape Cod
of blowing a hurricane into the dock.

In my despair I searched for the wisdom
that speaks through the cracks in certainty.

    *   *   *   *

Iver Johnson made a revolver, a .22
to shoot people with; Mr. Johnson spoke for me.

The Iver Johnson holds eight rounds,
when Grier jammed the hammer with his thumb

I had already emptied it
into the Jew loving senator from the East.

    *

They played politics over whether to kill me;
it made no difference, I had done with life;

I am the Palestinian Sirhan Sirhan
I killed Bobby of the Kennedy clan.

HER SUICIDE ON HIS BIRTHDAY

To the factory they bring the night's cull
the ritual of shoal fall;
he calls the scallop boy – wife!
a joke – bring the jute sacks, knife
the clams, it's my birthday!

Moving on, I must be moving on
I'm fucked with the monotony
the cranking mad-voiced escalator
belt with its own despotic litany reminding me
I am no more an idea than slime mould.

Behind the factory the mountains rise
without excuse or warning
damn the man! Damn the superman!

He knows he rose from a silt like the tar spit
of a dragon sated on coal.
It's time that defines ethic's mortmain
then, so soon, the better of good is vain.

She is the chopper of the savoy
the gatherer of the peel
the snipped locks of clay dolls;

before the fire she steams
from her soaking by the sea;
she looked out at that global lake
for an eye sparkle; for
the little pool fishing of childhood;
for a glimmer of the limby lad
who swept away her pooled anxiety
with lips anarchic like a little wave;
but all will mend, is mending on his birthday
with purpose and pursed lips
over the red blood-let onions

and then she dies;
I am dying she sighs as air comes to rest;
suddenly her knife
has split the world and all life
is falling into the ravine where dead dogs collect,
as though from a sky scraper in a dream
she only had once, has dropped rain
and, too soon the better of good is vain.

He leaves his mates flushed in the boiling velvet
blood of the Brazilian guitarist's tune
cold walker on the road of fits
with polka, ska and rigadoon
where lobsters and monk fish hang from trees
tortured by the inadequacy of eviction
sailing the sky of numbing seas
where the bats like salt wraps fiction
a rising to earth;
and love – the commanding screech owl –
is there at the midnight's birth
of desolation.
                    Home always makes him foul
when he's in his drink
but there amidst the clamour of autopsy
his heart doesn't sink
to discover in wedlock's biopsy
that she has gone to swim in sugar;
the machine's claw scrapes at his ego
he will never again fulfil his hate for her
no more the hit of night glow
never again feel the slipping away of pain
she is gone where more than good is vain.

FATHER

The patterns on the Corporation bus
window that might have seemed like Klimt etchings
were for him just frost. Cold.
He's going to the foundry to burn off the Winter.

Through the ice he recalls his war inside great seas
in wood hulled mine sweep
stoking the ship's knots.
Somewhere out on the cold street

a saxophone figure rises and he
has crossed the Sargasso
and the ripping wilderness of ocean
to the black peopled South

to some bayou bar to lose
his mind in a pleasure
to be always memorial. My
father was not a collector

of butterflies or comrades
in solidarity but collected memories that became a swamp in him.
Absurdly he emerged from
his many fathomed mine-charged

sea with a heart stupid for chrome;
expecting a silver-plated future
but the foundry got him
and he would cough up aluminium dust

with a howl like a crying saxophone
in the throat of his corpse.
In his sadness he had become
radicalised: a collector of platitudes and fears

wanting tearfully to be on the sea
a clown subject always to the back-stabbing waves.

DOGDREAMS

Our dog lives on a 4 x 4
island of blue blanket that used
to be our winter wrap.

I watch him; I can tell
by his sleeping whimpers
that he's enamoured of and exposed by
his Oriental fore-lives for his eyes
even in sleep
have a wise disposition
as though he were thinking:
a study of history will, frighteningly,
reveal how like a living room the world is.

I can see him as a pup in Shanghai
startled by an intuited fear
of the docks as a place
where every breed and culture
of dogs, brave and cowardly, brute
and weak is brought
for export by the exploiters of meek minds
where any amount of coercion and enforced
copulation to soften them up for exile is the norm;

and yet, as long as he can dream
a story there will have been the desire for love
and here's what creates the paradox
of doglife: that though he may dream:
O! if only I could ride a bike!
I would cycle the world
and unite dogs against dog slavery!
And I would commit any sin
or evil for that good! he would if he could
want to find that one bitch
– most likely a Pekinese –
who he would gladly let bring him humbled to his knees.

BICENTENNIAL

for Aberaeron

Chip away at the façade of Beau Nash
architecture to the bone ash mortar of birth
and as in the pulling of a sash
lift the veil that blurs sea with earth;

chronology too is blurred
by the successive exits
of those only heard
of in passing. Time's prerequisite

is that all will join the procession
of those ancient sea
travellers who wait before dawn on the discretion
of being to be

to have, in time, the invite dispensed
with as with Beau's men; those now quick and fast
in death who with prescience
built this town to last.

The cormorant years call and with resigned ease
we begin our slide into the arms of the sea,
but this year test the ancient breeze
across the cold harbour and be

amazed how, led by that ghost baritone
released from the suck of the sea's grave,
those of two centuries obliged to abandon blood and bone
(when you would think there was no sense to save)

are met on the elision of sea and earth
to sing with the fish that sing and fly
of this year of passion and rebirth
where yesterday touches tomorrow's sky.

GODIVA

It was in the days when I drove the truck.
I came to a town in a then unnamed country
and hit a jam which paralysed the traffic
for miles in every direction. I parked
my truck to investigate and in the town centre
found the cause: a beautiful woman
naked as the dawn on an enormous horse.

I went to a small café – clearly nothing
would be moving for a while and there I began
speaking with a young man who was, it seemed
to me, ostentatiously excited. He said
he'd just left a lecture on the poet
Keats in which he'd been overwhelmed by Keats'
innocent intemperance and had taken away with him
this resonance: that dissolution may once have been
found in a Latin hat with the self-consciousness
and purpose consequent on that.
                                    Then
he said: what did you think of her?
Her brave soft feathered flesh upon that coarse back;
it wasn't simply a gimmick!
it was the ace played to suck
out the resistance of anyone reluctant to serve.

I was unprepared for that. I said: surely
this is a romance; a kind of inverted Keats.
                        He laughed.
No, I said: you would be the Quaker killed
by the librarian's knife!

That evening we went drinking; how
clearly I remember later at his flat
bottle of wine between us, how his
erudition made my eyes sparkle
how I wanted to kiss him on the lips;
I imagined, as the grenache took hold
a bible the size of the floor
rolling with him on the pages of Ecclesiastes
indifferent to vanity as we brushed thigh on thigh.

That aristocratic Godiva with her
bare-fleshed arrogance
was always going to bring misery in her wake.
Hardly any time later
I found his body wrapped
in a bald sheet for the generals
who had effected his death like a poet would a stanza.

I was so angry I returned to the
town centre where the Godiva had performed
and I climbed the steps of a monument
to some vainglorious hero
and I shouted to the people there:
what was she for you? Some Brunhilde?
You gave in to her beauty and celebrity!
The ghost's handkerchief waves at her window
she has made of life the nightmare
dreams break from;
there is nothing but last breath
to cover the pots of flesh –
your child's hands in one, head in another;
all the golden eggs are black rocks
and the recommencing sea, re-becoming
with each wave, is irrelevant.

When I finished
there was silence. But it was hopeless.
In less than a minute someone shot me
through the head. I saw the bullet coming
for in that last moment of life
I had exceptional powers
like the innocent stripped of all compromise.

THE WOMANISER

In his eyes there is wilderness
this is death
her pupils are like the holes
in pitted olives
he'd come down a long road.

It had been a kind of poetry
the journey
the crying children
an alliteration
within irregular stanzas.

He'd been intruiged when the lines
didn't work: the pre-op transsexual;
it's in the flaws
you get the magic
in the broken drum
the dead beat.

But this was blood
the verses on the page swamped in it
like white bread in gravy.

It was over.
He'd borrowed too heavily
from the Jew in paradise
for there to be anything to collect
for the volumes he'd published
and any reviews he knew
would be redundant.

THE MOUNTAINEER

Each day in the city's market
around a bench of pine –
unwinding the scruples of clacks met
in assembly rooms with sublime

manifestos, fiats spilled over
from too full political cups –
are gathered the smokers, lovers
of the thin cigarillos, pups

of the dog fathers who themselves spun
sunlight into that filigree
of cod history which does not mention
their unfailing faltering. There is a holy

feel to these meetings: they collect
to commune but only the length of the smoke
then leave without respect
for the collective, the cloak

over their uncertainty fallen.
                    Today, as they leave, a man
with legs unbending like pitons
stalls to sit at the table, in hand
his Old Port smoke like a baton;

but he, unlike the recent departed
is not stalled in time but space
upon some peak uncharted
like the lines on a buried face.

AUDEN AND THE COCK

Auden stood and watched as the river dried
and all the unbettered flowering became
a white wilderness between voices.
He watched the truck lights traipsing
up the bloody valley;
ruts bleeding with slush
the bare tree shocked into its silhouette;
from dirt's bowels a silent bellow rose
and all the mad, diseased, crow-picked fish with it.

Auden imagines Vienna, the patched houses
and wilting trees; a tomb like a small mountain
where the moon visits as gravediggers rebury Mozart –
the commandatore come to cart off culture –
while Auden strokes his lover's
chlorine cock poised like a whiskey bottle
at his hip and hears the charcoal breath
over a tortured song and, tearful, laments
the intolerable loneliness of the intellect.

And now the poems have returned
to the trees, to the seas and to the hills
and the world has gone dark
and Highgate holds the death
of desirable futures and the women
remain in the kitchen to await feminism.

BUNTING

In memoriam Iraq

In the street they'd hanged
the teacher and the councillor
the tailor the jeweller the actor
the banker the landlord
the solicitor his secretary
the painter accountant estate agent
the cobbler bus driver the postman
restaurateur hairdresser professor
the hardware salesman fishmonger
butcher caretaker beggar
the baker the roadsweep the bin man
the lecturer the writer the waiter
the carer the doctor his nurse and the butcher;
in fact, a minor multitude who've
stiffened, brittle like pine trees or stars
and they've lit them
and the children cry out and clap
and the mothers sharing their joy
reflect with warmth inside
on how nice it is to go that little to excess
at this time of the year.

Me, I love my life
and that whole carnival of Christmas
but found it difficult to rise this morning
after last night's bacchanalia
and feel a little uncertain
about joining the world's traffic in the violet rain

ICEMAN

He wanted to be
involved with the theatre
in his small town by the sea
they said: you cannot speak our language

it was like a beheading

he experienced the suicidal impress
of air
the whistle of shells
over the pond of surf
in his head he heard
the high violin trills of hell
a music damaged by design
felt his hand tremble upon a haunted
heart string

he was the earth's last bird

they froze him out
and his head fell from him
in the tail wind
created by the emergency door he left by.

Headless, he became a seller
of refrigerators
a freezer by proxy
an iceman on a silver highway

but he wouldn't return to life in an age of ice
he saw his future
buried in the warm trenches of order
so, turgid middays
he would squander reading

and studying the fallopian
themes of bureaucracy
finding a language even theatre would submit to:

a graffiti daubed by despots on the heart

MORNING OF THE REVOLUTION

I read by lamplight of Praxiteles.
This was not part of a systematic
study of ancient art, I simply
couldn't sleep. It was the morning

of the revolution. More important was the cold:
an Arctic cold I wanted to suffer
to harden myself, prevailed in my room. It was
important that I didn't seem to

myself, let alone others, like
a desperado – a child emerging
from a dust of poverty
driven entirely by raggedness; that I was made of ice.

When it came, the overthrowing,
I felt like Shakespeare, shaping anew a culture;
there was no excuse for what had preceded
and no sentiment strong enough to justify remembering;

yet, ironically, despite my part in the eager
destruction of the past and present that followed that morning,
one thing that stayed with me through the days
of the terror to come (I was still cold)

was that, notwithstanding the successive
collapsings of recorded history
we know even today that Praxiteles' lost masterpieces
were ranked very highly by antiquity.

TO THE MUSEUM

Finding Yeats' tower in Clare
(like a monument to him)
made me ill.
I don't think it was the travelling

for I have always roamed; I used to be an itinerant;
and even then pursued the youthful aesthetic practice
of making love with the daisies
shooting into the earth
conceiving poems among the truffles.

I know that as I walked towards the tower from the car park
my heart beat sickeningly
and in my mouth the drying
of fall out from some elemental explosion;
you wouldn't have thought any man (or woman!)
could be so great that your recognition
of them could make you weak.

By the next morning I'd had enough;
into my room
light came through the dirty blind and in the gloom
seeing in my mirror my stupid
face and bodily form
as all the flesh there is, demanded of myself
and all I am, sublimation.

Down the hallway I hear
them coming for me with newspapers folded
to make batons
I run from my room as though the walls were on fire!
I am evicted from all that I thought
meant something; I am evicted for wanting
to take things seriously:
Yeats didn't have the holocaust or the bomb
to belittle his purpose.

Too much work, too much failure
has made me sick
picking on the borders
to claim just a grass blade of Elysium.

I ran and came to the museum as a refugee
ragged and determined as Raskolnikov
to sublimate my fever for art
even if only as a shiver on its wall
like a mark left by some uncontrollable child;
but the guardians of mediocrity have had their coup!
they're already here
they hold the doors
and take me as I enter
to a room where a disused presentation
of the origins of the Universe
is stored; they tie me
to a table spanning a billion years
freeze my eyes open
with a solution made from nuclear salt
and with a gleeful irony
torture me by dropping on my face
from a place in the clerestory (where they let the light in)
drip upon drip
the reconstituted blood of the masters.

FROSSO

Frosso came to us from Greek Cyprus
to our small town and
university – the smallest in Europe
she had been orphaned by indifference
schooled in private English schools
and now in her late teens was suffering
a fake reclaiming by her indifferent mother –
it was her mother who wanted her to come to Lampeter

I said: what do you want?
She said: I want to go to New York
I want to study Art not writing
but my father won't fly
if I'm in Lampeter he can sail from Cyprus.

I thought of Frosso's father a latter day
Ulysses sailing into a harbour on our
contentious coast.
                    I walked her through
our rare cloisters. I said:
and tomorrow, will you go back?
No, she said, Swansea.
I said: why Swansea? In the war it was
flattened and is now a city of
unpromising architecture. Do you know
about the second world war? O, yes, she
said. Hitler. I like Hitler. You like Hitler?
I thought of that English public school.
Yes, she said, he was smart. I said:
do you mean in the way he dressed?
(Lampeter's lack of designer outlets
had been a disincentive) No, she said,
he was smart. I like Sarkosi, too. I
recalled Mitterand – I thought he was smart –

he had gone from Right
to Left, now it's all the other way. As I left her
I said: what about Metaxas?
O, no! she said. He was Greek! And laughed.

THE BARGAIN

I'd empathised with
Kerouac on Desolation Peak
where watching for fires he'd met
the Buddha – a nebula
formed of the dust of his paradoxes;
Jack was made the god of youth
and it burnt him.

As we set out for our peak
in the declining day
desolation, at first, enraptured me:
we passed the ruins of mine works
and walked the stone art
of men of lordly presence
working men who'd faced the inescapable
quid pro quo
of feeding the machines that would
kill their children.

Coming to the mountain
is a movement into a history
where horror is a tic;

a wind gets up, a complex wind
that skins the cynic and shreds religion
it's a wind come from the icy plains of Greenland
we climb to where gods pay homage to sheep
there is no water save what you can carry on your back;

ordinarily we are tuned like trees
but here we are, at best, Aeolian harps
passive before the mountain's whistle
there is no end of death in these drifts
the effect is to numb like a skinning
we smell the breath

of a flesh eating deity
these gods despise the crawler;
de-sanctify the lick-spittle.

The wind speaks to me of ends and my rotting
we submit to nature
in order to process our dying
we are not even black sheep who will save their
godly white mates unseeable against the snow.

I met the mountain god
a glum god
fat with snow
I crawled through drifts into
his arms and in an eyeful of frosty air
he offered me release from my defence of failure;
comfort in anonymity and I took it.

(Kerouac had made his bargain with fame
and descended his
mountain to a future ruined by accomplishment.)

At sea level I thought of the
beautiful young whose adoration I'd
bargained away on the mountain;
thought with regret of the
quickening lay of age;
of being minnowed by the muscular young
and then there was stillness and dusk and in the stillness
I heard my wife's voice which reminded me
of Summer, of elms, of lawns and
wind chimes made of bone.

KIDS

If anyone said of my kids
that they were in manner, body or mind
in any way malformed, disturbed from this criterion
or that by some kind of miscreant development as though
that word miscreant is anyway a decent word to use about anybody
I'd say: if I could I would take you to the top of the red cliffs of Gramvousa
and leave you without nourishment until Ulysses comes round again.

It's the same with my poems:
don't tell me they don't meet some criterion of what's
done now in poetry as though they were malformed or miscreant
as if it's ever ok to use words like that to condemn other words as though
it's ever alright to use words to declare war on words as though words
were never

a symptom of some more pacific desire.

I embrace my kids and my poems as they embrace me
with love and trust and the occasional forgiven lapse into invective
and when I'm dead they will come to visit me at my tombside
as they may visit the tombsides of greater poets
who have written their battled for brilliant words on our hearts and faces
crucially arguing for mind as metaphor for death; and in that
the passing from the word into full-meaninged silence;

and when I'm dead they will meet me as mother moon meets the
waxing tide
that waxing of life and heart; meet me as the breeze meets flowerhearts
preparing pollen for the plenipotentic bee; for the heart will place
the last full word to the last pulse and beyond the leather
of the lexicon; they will meet me on the moorland where the bones
and spine
of debreasted creatures memorialise our passing and they
will love me for loving the hard climb; the uncertain step
and shifting gradient that degraded path to the heart
of the poem where arrival offers the offer of meaning

the shift from outer conjecture to inner and the offer of certainty
that lifts from pleasure to passion from the foothills to the summit

from childhood to maturity from the certainty of immortality
to the feather lift and fall of finality.

THE GIRL FROM IKARIA

Vasiliki, he said, you're
an Ikarian
you people just
fall
from the sky
and you don't care who you land on
because what you really want
is to reach
the sun. But you,
you have the sun
in your face. People – men – should be
flying
towards your beauty!
                    What about you, she said.
He said: I'm married!
Then she said:
so why quote
mythology
to me you
hopeless Christian!
And then she jumped
off the cliff
on which they were standing
and flew away.

THE BIRTH OF MORALITY

One evening, Xanthippe, Socrates' wife
while walking with her friend Alcestis
on the construction site of a new temple
to a minor god, stopped with the simple

woman to study the frieze of dancing marble just as
the dark, in fact, made sober
the Dionysian stone (as if to prepare
it for its Apollonian future)

when from the same entablature
fell a portion of it of disproportionate
importance onto Alcestis' head
killing her instantly. Totally. Dead.

Xanthippe returned home
with all the grieving of Euripides on her shoulders
to find Socrates entertaining a young turk.
She said: I need to talk.

Socrates said: this is Alcibiades,
Alcibiades this is my wife Xanthippe,
would you excuse us? Alcibiades left
and Xanthippe collapsed onto Socrates' breast, bereft:

such a show of affection, what brings it on?
Not affection, she shouted: fool!
She told the philosopher of the killing. O how I hate
that he said, but it is life, it's how we live; it's fate;

it is, dear wife, a tragedy. Tragedy! She cried, isn't tragedy
a theatrical form? It is, he said, and it is reality.
Well I want better than that for my friend!
I don't want her death to be a tragic end!

A tragic death would be so pointless and useless! Without
purpose. There is no purpose, said Socrates, there is
just living in a dangerous world the best we can;
all is contingency which is why, on any man

a brick may fall and end an otherwise marvellous
run. And what about good? said Xanthippe. Good?
said Socrates. How do you mean? Well, she said,
drying her eyes, I'm not sure – this is off the top of my head

but Alcestis was good and you'd think that there would
be, well, a residue of that goodness after her. For being good.
But where would that be? asked the sage
(as though a new youth could follow age!)

And what is this being good? he said.
Something may be good but what is *being* good?
Is it a new idea? Good is an adjective not an ideal
Get over your grief; wake up to the real!

Xanthippe withdrew from her husband. She said:
Do you think we *are* or are about to be?
Is this Heraclitus Xanth? She paced.
His cynicism, she felt, should be effaced.

No, no. Are we living now or only moving
towards some future point of being?
We are living *now*! Of course. That's axiomatic.
Then, she said, we are in a state of being: static

rather than…than, she hesitated…
Becoming? he asked succinctly.
Yes, she said, and if we live in a state of *being*
when things happen to us that is *part* of our being.

Yes, said Socrates. Well then, she said,
why can't we decide how we want to *be*?
It's becoming that's subject to chance; being
demands something more; more total like seeing –

vision, something that contains all we want to be.
But this itself is tragedy! sang the impatient Socrates.
You are attempting to find any chance
of avoiding submitting to fateful circumstance;

nothing is more tragic! No, no and no
shouted Xanthippe. Tell me – when you get
things intellectually wrong you put them right
using reason. You! I mean you! Reason! You fight

for it which makes us different from the goat – and
while we're on this, don't forget that the winner
of the play contest gets a goat as his prize – *tragos*: goat!
Tragoidia – tragedy! O how the cynics gloat!

which is an insult, a satire on the intellect:
our cultural masters want us to believe
there can be no purpose in intellectual
reasoning because it's all ultimately ineffectual

but do *you*, who reasons, believe in that: the supremacy of the gods!
as though they sent that marble to Alcestis' head?
It is we who should have supremacy as an objective
and we who should see good as more than an adjective!

Socrates drank deep of the wine Alcibiades
had brought. This *is* new, wife. Are you saying
that my need as a philosopher to put intellectual wrongs
right is a condition of something higher sung than those songs

of fate and that it's intellectually dishonest to hide behind
tragedy? Xanthippe answered: I knew you would find the right
way to say it. She paused. You said, she said,
that all we can do is attempt to live – lift your head! –

well in a dangerous world. Yes, said the tipsy man. And that
if we succeed in this, she said, that makes us happy.
Happiness, slurred Socrates is life's one identifiable
goal. But, Xanthippe contended, to her increasingly friable

spouse, can you really be happy not knowing what they'll throw
at you next? Wouldn't it be so much better if we could achieve
a happiness that wasn't conditional on the gods
not dropping bricks on us? Wouldn't that be *good*, god

– like itself? That would be good, he said, even if only as an adjective.
And wouldn't that kind of happiness, she said, be
transcendent? Hmmmm, he hummed, proceed.
Well, in that sense, she said, good would need

to be more than an adjective, it would be a value! And if this
good was transcendent it would be indestructible!
And this supreme value of good would contain *must*
contain all desirable goods and supersede all and just

as it is indestructible, so, when the marble block fell on
Alcestis, though her body was destroyed, the idea of
her which is her goodness, was not crushed and wasted.
Are you saying, said Socrates that the dead Alcestis

is something like a form of happiness? Xanthippe
replied, yes! Because the idea of her lives on in her
reflected good! Then surely, said Socrates now quite
drunk, her death is not a tragedy at all but a light

comedy. Yes, but a comedy in the sense that we have achieved
a harmony despite the spiteful gods. A harmony
that nothing can destroy. Sho, said Socrates, fundamentally
you're saying that somewhere there exists transcendentally

ideal forms of our most desirable needs that
you call the Good that we can all aspire to by being good.
Yes! Said Xanthippe. He paused: No sophist or cynic, no hedonist,
no Zeus loving poet or prophet or A list

thinker has ever or would ever moot
such rot, they'd boot him out of the agora
and you're wrong about your goat; the chorus
sung the life and death of Dionysus

and in this liturgy the singers
wore masks and what the *thiasotes* or *tragoi*
began, soon actors would impersonate:
the encounter of human will with fate;

to argue the birth of whatever it is you're arguing
would mean the death of tragedy
and I won't have it! (*Pause*) Then listen here, said Xanthippe
hovering menacingly over her lippy

spouse. Accept that the only god is *good*
and that Alcestis' death had meaning
and was not tragic nonsense, is that clear?
or you will never again welcome Alcibiades here.

And so, in that Grecian twilight at the end of antiquity
tragedy died, happiness and virtue became one;
good became God and Socrates conceded
that all that's passed had once preceded.